Finding God
in
Everyday Life

by
Rev. Kevin Coughlin

PAULIST PRESS
New York/Ramsey

Library of Congress
Catalog Card Number: 80-84506

ISBN: 0-8091-2351-7

Published by Paulist Press
545 Island Road, Ramsey, N.J. 07446

Printed and bound in the
United States of America

Contents

To C.F. Griffith,
my friend
and spiritual director
in college seminary days
who made Christ
real to me

Preface

Two not very well-known sentences from *The Pastoral Constitution on the Church in the Modern World* of the Second Vatican Council read as follows:

> Nor, on the contrary, are they any less wide of the mark who think that religion consists in acts of worship alone and in the discharge of certain moral obligations, and who imagine they can plunge themselves into earthly affairs in such a way as to imply that these are altogether divorced from the religious life. This split between the faith which many profess and their daily lives deserves to be counted among the more serious errors of our age (Art. 43).

The purpose of the following essays, accompanied by questions for reflection and an annotated bibliography, is to help the reader overcome the split mentioned by the Council Fathers between faith and everyday life.

The immediate origin of this book goes back to a Sunday evening in early October of 1978 when I shared some convictions on this theme with a group of forty to fifty adults in a city-wide adult religious education program in Prairie du Chien, Wisconsin. After that I used this topic for the beginning session of adult theology classes in parishes of the Diocese of Davenport. The topics for the remaining five sessions were selected by the adults involved in the classes.

Frank Wessling, a perceptive observer of human experience and a gifted writer for *The Catholic Messenger,* our diocesan paper, participated in one of these courses. After the first session he invited me to develop these ideas into seven columns for *The Messenger* during Lent of 1979. I was pleased to do this and somewhat gratified by the response to the columns. My thanks to Frank for the invitation. The present book represents a significant expansion of those columns.

During the time I wrote the columns I was also completing a doctoral dissertation for the Graduate Theological Union in Berkeley on the topic of the relationship between religious education and everyday experience. The material in this book is different from the dissertation. What unites the two is my long-standing interest in the religious dimensions of everyday life.

The real origins of this book go back a long way in my life story. Ever since my college days I have been uncomfortable with any implication that God and everyday life are two separate realms. Leo Tolstoy wrote, "To acknowledge God and to live are one and the same thing. God is what life is." When I first read those words, quoted by William James in *Varieties of Religious Experience,* I knew exactly what Tolstoy meant.

God's presence to all of life has been a central theme of my life and of my work in the priesthood. This book is by no means a final statement. It is but one step on a long journey.

May this step on my journey be helpful to others on theirs!

1   *The Treasure Is at Home*

I should like to speak of God
not on the borders of life
but at its center,
not in weakness
but in strength,
not, therefore, in man's suffering
      and death
but in his life and prosperity. . . .
God is the 'beyond' in the midst
      of our life.*

Once upon a time, there lived in Cracow, Poland a rabbi named Eisik who dreamed three times that there was a treasure buried beneath a particular bridge in Prague.

After the third dream, Eisik finally walked the long distance to Prague. When he found the bridge, the captain of the soldiers who were guarding it asked him why he had come. Eisik told him of his three dreams. The captain replied that if he had had faith in dreams he would have gone to Cracow a long time ago when he dreamed that there was a treasure buried in the ground under the stove of a Jew named Eisik.

*These words were written by a German Lutheran pastor, Dietrich Bonhoeffer in his *Letters and Papers from Prison* (New York: Macmillan, 1962), pp. 165–166.

When Rabbi Eisik heard this, he left immediately, walked the long journey home, and dug up the treasure underneath his kitchen stove.

We are all Rabbi Eisik. This tale from the Hasidic Jewish tradition, which dates back to the 18th century in central Europe, is about all of us.

The theme of this book is that God can be found in our everyday experience.

In Christian life, we can do special things or the usual things in a special way. Or both. This book suggests that the emphasis should be on doing the usual things in a special way.

Wisdom abounds in the Church's long tradition of emphasizing penance and fasting, particularly during the season of Lent. We could all be more aware, caring, supportive, forgiving, and grateful than we usually are. Asceticism, one of the basic realities of the spiritual life, doesn't mean only rigorous self-denial. Sometimes when people hear of asceticism they think of long fasts, hair-shirts, and scourgings. Asceticism also means taking responsibility for dispensing with anything that gets between us and God.

One of those things that gets in the way might be the attitude that God is found only or mainly in places, acts, and words which are labeled "religious."

No one has to look very far for penance in his or her life. There is penance enough built right into the ways and structures of modern life: driving through bumper to bumper traffic, being subjected to noise of one sort or another almost constantly, recognizing the need to conserve energy by keeping room temperatures low and driving less, etc. When the right intention or attitude is present, penance can be doing the ordinary things in an unusual way, a way through which we discover God.

Another of the things that can get between us and God is the attitude that we turn to God only when we feel a serious need or are in a time of crisis. People frequently say that they turn to God only when they have a problem. An Irish priest said at a clergy day a few years ago that grace only comes through suffering. If this position were correct (and it is not), then we should all try to suffer as much as possible. This would be religious masochism.

God comes through good times too. We need to learn to be with God when we are feeling happy, excited, and content. Prayers of thanksgiving and praise are as valid as prayers of petition. The beauty of a face, a painting, a plant, and a piece of music is a reflection of the beauty of God. In the Old Testament, there are psalms of thanksgiving and praise as well as petition. God can be discovered in the good times as well as the bad.

The experience of people is important, much more important than is usually realized. This is true because our experience is the center of whatever God is saying to us. Theologian Bernard Cooke writes that experience, particularly in some form of community (in the family, for most people), is the externalization of the Spirit. Our experience is the temple of the Spirit.

Though it might not seem so, this emphasis on experience is quite traditional. It is only in recent centuries that experience has become suspect, particularly to many religious leaders. For some people, experience is a devil-term, one which is full of negative meanings.

Yet, in the Old Testament, the Greek and Hebrew terms for knowledge mean coming to know through experience. Knowledge in this sense is another word for sexual intercourse. Thus, to know a woman is to engage in sexual intercourse with her. For St. John the Evangelist, to know is concrete experiential knowledge and for St. Paul, the contact between Christ and the Christian is experiential. The New Testament did not come from a divine "hotline." It came from the early Church reflecting on its experience of

Christ which was synonymous with reflecting on its own life. Doctrines, frequently absolutized by those who denigrate experience, are simply conceptualizations of the Church's experience.

Again, today, experience is becoming a central concern. Most theologians consider it to be an important source for their reflecting and that is why they are listening to people, studying other disciplines, and taking cultural contexts seriously.

Most psychologists describe the healthy person as one who moves away from the pole of defensiveness toward the pole of openness to experience. Whole movements, *est*, for example, are thriving with the goal of assisting people to experience consciously what they experience. People who don't trust their experience, who are not in touch with it, and who suppress it usually end up with serious difficulties of one sort or another.

One aim of religious faith is to help people overcome estrangement—separation or disconnectedness—from their own experience.

Everyday experience deserves to be taken seriously both because it is everyday and because it is experience.

The emphasis in much official talk is on finding God mainly through membership in the Church, participation at Sunday Mass, or involvement in formal religious education programs. The attempt is made to limit God to formal religion.

Because the religious realm is broader and deeper than institutional religion, this talk doesn't always ring true to the experience of people. However helpful these formal places are for some, they are not the only places to find God.

Some people find God through shoveling snow from the sidewalk of an elderly neighbor, a loving act of sexual intercourse, being forgiving toward a recalcitrant son or daughter, trying to inform themselves and decide practically what can be done about the enormous problem of world hunger, or even dancing ecstatically to new wave music.

There are not two separate realms, one called God and the other called the world, which depend upon us to relate them to each other. Our knowledge and experience of God are mediated by the world in a permanent, ongoing manner throughout our lifetimes. We are not here to transcend the world now for something higher. Jesuit theologian William Dych writes, "The more one keeps both feet solidly on the ground, the better one can find God, and even to try to keep one foot in heaven and one foot on earth is to run the risk of being painfully pulled apart."

God can be found within our human experience, our own everyday life. To find God we do not need to leap out of the world but to pass through it. This passage, which is the journey of our life, involves taking responsibility for the condition of the world. Working to make the world more humane, we become more human. The way to God is not "up" to the heavens but "down" to the depths of life. Dych again, ". . . the very sensibility which enables us to live in and interact with the world in a truly human way is the very sensibility which enables us to see God."

People do not have to bring God to themselves or to the world. Some think that if they do certain religious acts (the more, the better, of course) God will come to them.

God is already here in the midst and the depths of our lives, our world, and our history. We do not have to bring God here as much as we need to recognize his presence already among us.

A good resolution, within the reach of everyone, is to begin digging up the treasure—in its various manifestations—beneath our kitchen stoves. This book will try to help.

Questions for Reflection

Note: The questions below and at the end of each chapter might serve the same purpose as the old examination of conscience. They are not questions which can be answered easily or quickly. Perhaps some cannot be answered at all. It is suggested that the reader select a question for each day. Let it be with her/him in different moods and at different times of the day. Perhaps a husband and wife could talk about these questions together. If a particular question begins to "hurt" a bit, then real reflection is taking place.

1. What particular attitudes do you have toward your everyday life?

2. To what degree do you trust your own experience?

3. Where do you tend to locate God most of the time?

4. What are the "treasures beneath the kitchen stove" in your life?

5. Do you acknowledge God in the good times as well as the hard times?

6. Do you tend to limit the religious realm to religion or to explicit religious words, acts, and events?

7. Think of a recent time when you experienced God as involved in something you did. Was it inside a church building or outside of it?

Bibliography

Baum, Gregory, *Man Becoming* (New York: Seabury, 1979), $8.95 paperback.
Subtitled "God in Secular Experience," this important theological work presents developments in our understanding of God and connects these to church, sacraments, Christ, the last judgment, morality, evil, and prayer. A basic premise is that "the sacred as the celebration of the depth dimension of human life enables men to lay hold of the ordinary daily reality in a new way."

Howard, Thomas, *Splendor in the Ordinary* (Wheaton: Tyndale House, 1977), $2.95 paperback.
Episcopal professor of English at Gordon College, Howard reflects on the home as the "domestic Church" (Vatican II, Lumen Gentium, 11). He presents a theology of the blueprint of a tract home with each room representing a different aspect of our universal priesthood: the kitchen for service, the bathroom for cleansing, the living room for the joy of mere being together, the entryway for the hallowing of comings and goings, and the bedroom for the deep mysteries of love-making, conception, birth, sleep, sickness, and death.

O'Meara, Thomas, *Loose in the World* (New York: Paulist Press, 1974), $1.45 paperback.
Dominican theologian Thomas O'Meara considers the necessity for and the difficulty of faith in our cultural context and presents an interpretation of God as presence. He reflects on various forms of explicit presence (Jesus, church, Bible, etc.) and urges that we not mistake it for the deeper and wider presence, the universal gesture of God called implicit presence. From this perspective, "everything 'religious' is secondary, if by religion we mean creeds and dogmas, rituals and rites."

Vann, Gerald, *The Water and the Fire* (London: Fontana
Books, 1961), paperback.
The late, prophetical Dominican theologian, Gerald Vann,
after perceptively analyzing the world of today, suggests the
importance of a symbolic way of looking at life and calls for
the recovery of love, nature, community, and an affirma-
tion of matter. The influence of Jung and great novelists
and poets is present throughout this book which clearly
merits republication in the United States as a contemporary
classic in spiritual writing.

2   *Finding God Through Self*

> . . . there is only one problem on which
> all my existence, my peace and my happiness depend:
> to discover myself in discovering God.
> If I find Him I will find myself and
> if I find my true self I will find Him.*

Chicago newspaper columnist Sydney Harris, a wise man if there ever was one, wrote several years ago that the human person is not like an apple that has to be polished but like a banana that has to be peeled.

Some people (Harris wrote "most people") spend their lives polishing by shining the surface (i.e., appearance, clothes, house in the "right" neighborhood, flashy car, etc.), and by perfecting the image (i.e., selling the package and not the product). The result of too much polishing and too little peeling is that people remain far from one another and never communicate or interact in any real way.

When polishing becomes an ever-present concern, as it seems to be with many people, the real person never comes to life, never reveals himself, never even knows himself,

---

*These words were written by Thomas Merton, the Trappist monk, who integrated psychological insights, Zen Buddhism, and a concern for justice in the world with his monastic life. They are from his *New Seeds of Contemplation* (New York: New Directions, 1972), p. 36.

and dies without ever having found his true existence. The false person dominates and wastes an entire lifetime.

Sunday Masses, promotions at work, academic degrees earned, adult education programs, salary increases, etc.—none of these will make much difference to us and to others until the peeling process, which takes a lifetime, is well underway. Work, liturgical ritual, learning, and relationships take on reality and new meaning in the sobering context of the peeling process which is another way to describe the journey from the false to the real self.

God wants us to peel, to get rid of our false selves, and to remove the distance between our outer and inner selves. In short, more than anything else, God wants us to become more human.

God wants us to do this because becoming our real selves is a way, perhaps *the* main way, to find him.

In his study of Thomas Merton's spirituality, James Finley describes the spiritual life in these terms: "the long and often arduous journey on which we slowly become detached from our false, illusory self—a self that is little more than the collective evaluations and affirmations of our surroundings—and are opened up to receive a new self that is participation in the life of God." Our true self is in communion with God. That is why finding it is finding God.

This emphasis grounds the spiritual life in the real world. The spiritual life has to do with being more than doing. It is not so much doing special things to become more holy as it is becoming more fully the persons we were meant to be.

God is there not only at the end of this life-long process of peeling. He is there all along the way. In fact, God is the drive, the direction, the support, and the energy of the whole process.

Numerous are the ways to say this. Some speak of transformation, dying to the old self and finding the new self, realizing the true self, finding one's deepest center, and becoming one with God. The late psychologists Abraham Maslow and Carl Jung wrote of self-actualization and individuation, respectively.

Controversial theologian Hans Küng states that God's cause is man's cause and that God's will is man's well-being. Another theologian, Gregory Baum, writes that God is redemptively present in the very process by which people become more present to themselves.

They are all talking about the same reality. It doesn't matter much what terms a person uses to describe this process as long as he is able to identify it in his experience of everyday life.

People really have no choice of whether or not to be involved in this process. Through birth, it becomes the fate of everyone. The choice is whether or not the process is recognized and how well or poorly the peeling is being accomplished. This is no small choice. Our salvation—our real person's health and wholeness—ultimately depends upon it.

What does it mean concretely to become more human or be more present to ourselves?

There's no doubt about the fact that it is hard to talk about. It means different things at different times to different people. It means different things at different times to the same person.

It might mean getting in touch with what is really going on inside of us. (The wife who feels and acknowledges for the first time the hurt that she has denied and repressed for a long time.)

Or uncovering our real motivations. (The college student who quietly admits to himself that he really didn't want to get drunk last Friday night and did so only because he was afraid to be different from his buddies.)

Or being willing to make a growth-choice which involves risk. (The man who decides, after so many years in a certain job, that he is not happy in that position and now wants to do work which is more satisfying personally to him.)

Or opening ourselves to another person. (The woman who finally tells her friend how much she likes her and how much she appreciates her friendship.)

Or reflecting on the connection between religious faith and real life. (The man who suddenly awakens to the realization that his receiving Communion at Sunday Mass has something to do with the way he treats his employees and customers.)

Or becoming a little less detached from our egos. (The person who has been preoccupied with what other people think of him and with what impression he is making comes to realize that it is not so all-important after all.)

Or becoming "unstuck" from a position that we have absolutized. (The person who for the first time begins to realize that there are other valid interpretations of a particular issue and that her interpretation is not the only one.)

Such realizations and acts are the basic stuff of the peeling process which happens under many different guises. Sometimes they can be dramatic; most of the time they are not. They usually happen gradually and not all at once. They usually happen in the hustle and bustle or the calm and quiet of everyday life.

The churches no longer possess a monopoly, if they ever did, on inward transformation or the peeling process. Jesuit theologian David Toolan writes, ". . . it is one of the distinctive marks of the modern age that the arts of tapping into deep spiritual reserves are no longer confined to church and its custodians, but widely distributed throughout our society. . . . The disciplines of remembering and rebirth have indeed taken on 'secular' form—and with the right attitude nearly anything will serve, from pottery and motorcycle maintenance to psychotherapy and Alinsky organizing." However one interprets what is or is not happening in the institutional Church, there is no cause for despair.

Regardless of the leadership, the priorities, and the quality of community life in a local parish or diocesan church, God continues to be present to life and people continue to grow. It would be quite wonderful, however, if the structures, programs and regular liturgies of the everyday life of the Church could more directly and effectively connect with the peeling or humanization process of those involved.

Some further examples. Take the growing interest in health. Many people are starting to take care of their bodies by eating more nutritious foods and getting regular exercise. For many, this amounts almost to a rediscovery of their bodies and is connected closely to the growth of the whole person. It's another way to be more present to oneself.

Take the women's awareness movement. (This is not necessarily the same in all respects as Women's Liberation.) Some women are starting to feel that they are not inferior to men, that they can assert what they want, and that their role in life need not be confined to mother and homemaker. It's another way of getting in touch with self.

Such peeling or becoming more human doesn't happen only or even mainly through social movements, though such movements are often a way that God manifests himself through the process of history. It usually happens through the ordinary processes of life: relationships, reflection, marriage, parenting, etc. For example, some people experience their aging process as a way to worship God—with decisions to keep interested in things outside of themselves, to shun self-pity, and to avoid bitterness.

But this is secular humanism or mere psychology, some will say.

It is not "mere" anything because a right understanding of religion celebrates persons becoming more human and regards God as the transcendent source of this humanization—with God located deep within rather than outside the person.

The main message of Jesus, the theme which summarizes all that he said and did, is "Repent and be glad; the Kingdom of God is at hand" (Matthew 4:17). This is a call to conversion, a call to all of us. The conversion of someone to the Catholic Church is a limited and non-biblical use of the word. Christ is calling us to something very basic, a fundamental turning about, a radical transition from the old person to the new person or from the false self to the true self. Christ is calling us to the peeling process.

James Finley describes this process in an intriguing, mysterious, and memorable story: "It is like the experience of a man who, while out walking alone on a bitter cold and starless night, unexpectedly comes upon a large, warm-looking house. Upon approaching the house and pressing his face against the window, he sees himself sleeping comfortably before the fire! Suddenly, he realizes that he is trapped outside his own house. He realizes his life is rich, yet he stands impoverished. He is secure yet he stands on the edge of death. He is fulfilled yet he stands sterile and empty.

"Frantically, he begins to pound upon the window, yelling loudly to be let in. But the self inside does not hear and, as he pounds, the glass barrier dividing him from his life only grows thicker and his clenched fists grow numb with pain.

"At long last, realizing finally that all efforts of brute force achieve nothing, he sits quietly in the snow overcome by a growing single silent desire, by an unfaltering hope, that he might be one with himself. This desire, though appearing powerless, awakens the self within and with this awakening the glass itself dissolves. The house dissolves

20

and he discovers that he was really at home all along and did not know it."

All of us are like the man standing outside of his own house. All of us can be less like apples and more like bananas.

Anytime is a good time to give attention to how well our own peeling—and emerging—process is coming along.

Questions for Reflection

1. How much time and energy do you give to "polishing" yourself?

2. How much time and energy do you give to "peeling" yourself?

3. What terms or phrases do you use to describe the life-long process of "becoming more human" or "becoming more real"?

4. Think about and list some significant events in this process of peeling in your life thus far.

5. Why is the matter of "becoming more human" so important to God? What are the connections between "becoming more human" and God?

6. How present are you to yourself most of the time?

7. What are three specific things that you might do to become less like an apple being polished and more like a banana being peeled?

Bibliography

Dunne, John S., *The Reasons of the Heart* (Notre Dame: University of Notre Dame Press, 1979), $4.95 paperback.
The basic premise of this book is that by coming to ourselves, through a journey of the human heart which goes out to meet loneliness in solitude and then comes back again to meet loneliness in the human circle, we come to God. Quoting Kierkegaard, Dunne writes, "That is how I propose to begin—by going out into solitude 'where nothing happens,' hoping there to experience things 'more perfectly, more precisely, more profoundly.'" The book demonstrates how, when the reasons of the heart become known to the mind, insight occurs.

Finley, James, *Merton's Palace of Nowhere* (Notre Dame: Ave Maria Press, 1978), $2.95 paperback.
Subtitled, "A Search for God Through Awareness of the True Self," this book explores the spiritual writings of Thomas Merton, particularly the theme of ultimate human identity. When the relative identity of the ego is taken to be the deepest and only identity then a person makes his empirical identity into the false self. The true self, which is our whole self before God, is realized only in the mode of simple awareness—the prayer of contemplation—proper to it. The chapters trace the journey from "the foundation of the false self" to the "realization of the true self."

Fromm, Erich, *To Have Or To Be?* (New York: Harper & Row, 1976), $12.95 hardback.
The main position of this book is that two modes of existence are struggling for the spirit of humankind: the having mode which concentrates on material possession, acquisitiveness, power, and aggression and is the basis of such universal evils as greed, envy, and violence and the being mode

22

which is based in love, in the pleasure of sharing, and in meaningful and productive rather than wasteful activity. Texts from the Old and New Testaments and from 14th century mystic Meister Eckhart are used to support the basic position. Because this book is not explicitly religious, it is a fine example of secular spirituality.

Rogers, Carl R., *On Becoming a Person* (New York: Houghton Mifflin, 1970), $4.25 paperback.

From the perspective of humanistic rather than behavioral psychology, this work describes the process of becoming a mature person and suggests the implications of this process for education, therapy, and family life. Rogers claims that experience is the highest authority for him, enjoys discovering order in experience, and defines the good life, in part, as a process involving an increasing openness to experience.

3 *Finding God Through Others*

> . . . God's presence is discernible in the ordinary
> situations of human life, in the dialogue that
> constitutes man's history and in the gifts that reconcile
> him with himself and with others. . . . The locus of the
> divine is the interpersonal.*

The only way to God is through each other.

Yes. There is no direct road to God. There is no road
to him that does not pass through our neighbor. And to
Christ, our neighbor is everyone.

Is this the extreme opinion of a humanist, a religious
socialist, a radical theologian, or a fuzzy-minded do-gooder?

No. It is exactly what the New Testament says in several places.

Take Matthew 25:40: ". . . I tell you, indeed, whenever
you did this for one of these poorest brothers of mine, you
did it for me!" This is the "punch line" of a story we have
all heard numerous times. Response to a hungry or sick person,
a stranger or a prisoner (and there is no need to be literal
about these categories: what is meant is anyone in

---

*These words were written by the Canadian theologian Gregory Baum in
a book which was one of the most influential theological works of the 1970's:
Man Becoming (New York: Herder & Herder, 1970), p. 58.

need) is response to Christ. The grounds on which the last judgment will take place—in other words, our salvation—is our response to each other.

Take James 1:27: "This is what God the Father considers to be pure and genuine religion: to take care of orphans and widows in their suffering, and to keep oneself from being corrupted by the world." In other words, "genuine religion" is not primarily going to church, obeying the Pope on birth control, refraining from sexual sins, and contributing to the support of your parish. Again, a literal interpretation gets us nowhere in a country with few orphans. Such an interpretation can even be an escape. "Genuine religion" is taking care of the social outcasts of our time (who are they? divorced people, handicapped people, gay people, minorities, ugly people, women frequently, emotionally disturbed people, alcoholics, etc.), as Christ did those of his time and reflecting on whether our values have been shaped more by advertising, television, and Hollywood than by the Gospel of Jesus Christ.

Take 1 John 4:20: "If someone says, 'I love God,' yet hates his brother, he is a liar. For he cannot love God, whom he has not seen, if he does not love his brother, whom he has seen."

Add Matthew 5:21–24, 1 John 1:6–7, 1 John 3:17, Romans 13:8–10, 1 Corinthians 13, Galatians 5:14 (as well as the many texts which document God's preference for mercy toward one's neighbor—the non-literal interpretation: everyone—even before the worship of God himself: Matthew 9:13, 12:1–8, 15:1–9, 23:23–24, etc.), and there is plenty of New Testament support for the position that we find God through each other.

It is strange, when this is such a consistent theme of the New Testament, that many people still conceive of the love of God mostly in a vertical contrasted with a horizontal way, one which leads directly from the individual to God.

An example of this is a somewhat common attitude toward the Mass. Many people see the Mass as an act of devotion mainly between themselves as individuals and God. They don't see the communal dimension of it: the Mass is people breaking bread and sharing the cup with each other. As people come to experience the Mass as an expression of community life (and not as an independent cult of individuals) they will come to realize that we find God through each other.

Because this position is based in the New Testament, it is not really an old Church-new Church issue or a liberal-conservative debate. The implication of it is not that all Christians, if they are true to Christ, must join sensitivity training groups, march on picket lines, make political action all important, and forget about involvement in the church, celebration of the sacraments, and formal prayer.

This point, however, does shed some light on the issue of how people who are not in the church or who have left the church are saved.

Many are the ways of finding God through others and some of them—perhaps most—are quiet, low key and part of the ordinary fabric of family and social life itself.

Relationships are the most effective "classrooms" in life. They teach us far more than books, schools, adult education classes, priests, and workshops do. The main way that a person learns about herself, others, life, and God is through involvement with others—and this is why there is no contradiction between the main point of the previous chapter and this one. A person cannot grow and become more human all by herself. It happens only through relationships. Martin Buber is right: to be is to be related.

Husbands and wives can reveal God to each other. The deepest revelation a wife receives of God's love is her experience of her husband's love. In the experience of loving his wife, a husband gives insight into the fact that God gives himself to us. Theologian Bernard Cooke writes, ". . . the husband causes the wife's grace, and the wife causes her husband's."

Parents can reveal God to their children. My own father taught me more about God than any book, religion class, priest, nun, or theologian and he did this without ever talking about God. He did this by the interest, trust, affection, freedom, and forgiveness he gave to me. A mother teaches a baby about God in the first hours and days after birth by holding the infant close to her, looking into his eyes, and thereby telling him non-verbally that his world is safe and trustworthy. An old saying goes, "God couldn't be everywhere and so he created mothers."

Parents are helping a child to come to know God through building a positive self-concept in her. Belief in God is rooted in positive feelings toward self and life. This is why the early years are very important in the religious education of a person. Protestant pastor-theologian Horace Bushnell wrote quite prophetically in the middle of the 19th century "that more, as a general fact, is done, or lost, by neglect of doing, on a child's immortality, in the first three years of his life, than in all his years of discipline afterwards."

The love between a father and a mother is one of the most important experiences a child ever has. It becomes a part of his own experience, understanding, and valuing of relationships. This is why parents do something important for children when they improve their own relationship by for instance, making a Marriage Encounter or taking time for themselves to be alone now and then. For the sake of their children and themselves, parents need to see themselves more often as persons with their own needs and not always in their role as parents.

Community always has been and still is today the privileged context for the revelation and experience of God. That's theory, to some extent. The hard practical question for almost everyone is: Where is the experience of community in my life? For most people it will be in the family, though there are other possibilities.

The most serious challenge facing the Church today is the need to make local parishes more credible. That means, most of all, making parishes places where people experience real community. The first practical step in building community is for people to get to know each other which includes, though is not limited to, the priest and people getting to know each other. Until this happens, all the guitars, parish councils, and deacons in the world won't make much difference. The main reason that Cursillo, Teens Encounter Christ, and charismatic groups have thrived at various times is that the people involved feel they are part of a community, however fleeting the experience may be.

It is not so much that building community in local parishes has failed. It has hardly been tried and won't be in a real way until the monopoly of ministry by the ordained priesthood is broken. The local parish will not be a community until people come to see themselves as the Church and realize that the call to ministry is based primarily in their baptism.

Some people find God through political action of various sorts. The world takes care of us by providing food, natural resources, beauty, wilderness, etc. If it is to continue doing this, we need to take better care of it by becoming more conscientious caretakers of planet Earth.

Striving for social justice and fighting social evils (Bob Dylan sings on his *Slow Train Coming* album, ". . . the enemy I see wears a cloak of decency . . .") are signs of the spiritual life as much as, perhaps more than, engaging in private religious devotions. In fact, the late Secretary General of the United Nations, Dag Hammarskjold wrote, "The way to holiness in our times is through the search for justice." To do this effectively depends on basic information, among other things. For the person who cares about what's happening in the world and tries to do something about it, the daily newspaper can become a prayer book of sorts.

It's comparatively easy, and a bit childish to "give up" certain things, such as candy, booze, cigarettes, etc., for Lent, though sometimes this can represent enormous penance for adults. It would be more fitting, although harder, for adults to do this: Make a basic review of the key relationships in your life and "give up" whatever keeps you from finding God more fully through them. It's really the only way to find yourself as well.

Questions for Reflection

1. Do you think of your love for God mainly in horizontal or vertical terms?

2. To what extent have your values been shaped by advertising, television, and Hollywood? To what extent have they been shaped by the Gospel of Jesus Christ?

3. What influence did your parents have on the formation of your image of God?

4. What have you learned about God from your husband, wife, or best friend?

5. Have you ever experienced the daily newspaper as "a prayer book of sorts"?

6. To what extent do you experience community in your local parish?

7. Give three examples of evil in the world today which "wears a cloak of decency."

Bibliography

Briggs, Dorothy Corkille, *Your Child's Self-Esteem* (Garden City: Doubleday, 1975), $2.95 paperback.
This work suggests that the ability of parents to develop healthy self-esteem in their children is the norm of good parenthood. High self-esteem is based on a child's belief that he is lovable and worthwhile. Every child builds his self-picture from the words, body language, attitudes, and judgments of others. Increasing their own self-acceptance allows parents to be more accepting of their children. In practical terms this book helps parents to build self-esteem in themselves and their children.

Capon, Robert Farrar, *Bed and Board* (Austin: S & S Press, 1977), $1.95 paperback.
Subtitled "Plain Talk about Marriage," this book by an Episcopal priest-theologian covers the topics of weddings, images, roles, bed, board, things, roots, and children with insight and pleasure. To parents, regarding children, Capon writes, "Delight in them openly. Speak your praise of them. Be their priest. Look at them with the widest eyes you can manage, and don't be ashamed to be seen at wonder . . . What a shame if they should leave without ever knowing they have been beheld and offered up by an astonished heart."

Ginott, Dr. Haim G., *Between Parent and Child* (New York: Avon, 1973), $1.75 paperback.
This book helps parents to understand their children's feelings. Offering concrete suggestions for dealing with daily situations, it presents new approaches to conversation with children, praise and criticism, expression of anger, achievement of independence, and the assumption of responsibility. Realistic dialogues are presented which illustrate how to behave when a child misbehaves. Words and phrases are

presented which exemplify good communication between parent and child.

Marstin, Ronald, *Beyond Our Tribal Gods* (Maryknoll: Or-
    bis 1979), $5.95 paperback.
The main thesis of this book is that responding to the cry of the poor and oppressed is not an option for the Christian but a constitutive dimension of maturing faith. Obedience to God involves the collective task of remaking the world. "Faith is the self as the self owns up to its most basic loyalty." The book considers how faith develops, how it gets sidetracked and how it is related to community, justice, and affluence.

4 *Finding God Through Things*

I believe a leaf of grass is no less than the
    journey-work of the stars,
And the pismire is equally perfect, and a grain of sand,
    and the egg of the wren,
And the tree-toad is a chef-d'oeuvre for the highest,
And the running blackberry would adorn the parlors of
    heaven,
And the narrowest hinge in my hand puts to scorn all
    machinery,
And the cow crunching with depress'd head surpasses
    any statue,
And a mouse is miracle enough to stagger sextillions of
    infidels.*

A bed, a book, a flute, a window, a tree, a stereo pho-
nograph, a tool, a house plant, a table, a jacket, a pear, a
star, an electric light, a telephone, a pair of Levi's, an onion,
a house and on and on.

These things serve us. The great American poet, Walt
Whitman called things "dumb, beautiful ministers." He
meant every thing in the world, but particularly those phys-

*These words were written by Walt Whitman in his famous book, *Leaves
of Grass,* in the 31st section of the poem, "Song of Myself." from *Complete Poetry
and Selected Prose of Walt Whitman* (Boston: Houghton Mifflin, 1959), p. 46.

ical objects he saw on his daily cruise on the East River in New York City. Addressing things directly Whitman said, "You furnish your parts toward eternity, Great or small, you furnish your parts toward the soul." In another place Whitman wrote of "the impalpable sustenance" which he derived "from all things at all hours of the day."

Things minister to us. They are both silent messengers from God and still pathfinders to him. The late 14th century mystic, Julian of Norwich looked at a little thing, a hazel nut, and, through viewing it attentively, realized aspects of God. If we have a right relationship to them, things in our everyday lives become transparent: we see them and, through them, we see much more.

Hasidic Jews believed that in creating the world God shattered himself and scattered his splendor in hidden sparks which are present in every thing and every possibility. Our work is the redemption of the divine sparks and the reunification of the whole. We do this when we approach any thing or situation with an attitude of presence, when we respond with our whole being to the unique claim of unique situations, and when we bring ourselves with all our possibility of response into every action. When we are really present to a thing, the divine sparks in it are released. By the quality of our presence, we transform the world and, in the terms of Hasidism, "hallow the everyday."

Our ability to be present, something which is hard to describe, will influence the degree to which we discover God through things.

Presence is really being in the here and now which is sometimes the hardest place of all for us to be. It is heightened awareness. When a person is really present, her mind is still and her perceptions are clear. She sees well, deeply, and through things. Presence involves detachment because when a person is detached from her own needs, desires, and fantasies, she is able to be with things and people in their own right.

To the degree a person is present, he can overcome the tendency to categorize, judge, compare, and mentally manipulate. Presence liberates people from expectations and preconceived experiences. When a person is present, his mode of knowing is receptive, patient, and relaxed. Presence is related to a main theme of *est* which is simply: "Pay attention and take what you get."

Being present to things is one way to the presence of God and when we are present to God we discover the deepest meaning of all things. It is no small art to be able to uncover the presence of things present. The spiritual life is the struggle to be present; it is a presence to be lived.

For most of his life, Jesus was a village craftsman. This means, among other things, that he worked with things: wood and tools. Who knows what lessons Jesus learned from these things? He must have noticed things well and been really present to them because frequently in his public ministry Jesus asks his listeners to let the ordinary things and events of their everyday lives become the means for understanding and accepting the activity of God.

Parables are Jesus' most characteristic form of teaching and are among the most authentic strata of the New Testament. After all, Jesus was not a priest, theologian, or interpreter of the law. He was a storyteller. Frequently his parables dealt with things: the fig tree, salt, coins, a grain of mustard seed, oil lamps, money, sheep, goats, vineyards, etc.

Parables and all metaphor, which is when one thing is spoken of as if it were another, can move us to see our ordinary world in an extraordinary way. Whether from the past or present, parables assume that important things happen and are decided at the everyday level. The language of parables does not take us out of everyday reality but drives us more deeply into it. Theologian Sallie TeSelle writes, "We do not live in a secular world that must be discarded when we become 'religious,' nor do we live in a 'religious' world which has no truck with the secular."

God is with us—which is the basic meaning of Emmanuel—in our human, everyday world. Incarnation means exactly this. To miss the earthiness of God is to miss the full reality of Jesus Christ.

How do we go about seeing our ordinary world in an extraordinary way?

One approach (there are several) is to consider the way that the things around us in our daily lives minister to us when we are attentive and present to them. If we see things well enough, we will see through them to new meanings.

Things can "speak" to us. That is why Francis Ponge called his little classic, *The Voice of Things* (New York: McGraw-Hill, 1974). In it he describes how rain, blackberries, a candle, an orange, a door, bread, snails, moss, a cut of meat, a pebble, among other things, "speak" to him. In Buddhism there is always communication of some sort going on between the human mind and material things.

Things can be felt as gifts from God. When this happens they are accompanied with feelings of gratitude. It is better to say grace at meals because the food before one looks, smells, and is good than it is for custom's sake alone. St. Francis of Assisi noticed things (sun, fire, moon, wind, and water) and connected them to himself and to God. He experienced such oneness with things that he called them "Brother" and "Sister."

Things can be a source of insight. St. Thomas Aquinas said that his source of insight was in little, sensible things. The late Abraham Heschel, a noted Jewish theologian, reflected the Hasidic tradition when he wrote of feeling "the hidden love and wisdom in all things." Painter Andrew Wyeth can never get close enough to or inside an object enough because for him there are always new revelations coming out of things. Whitman wrote that "all truths wait in all things." For another American poet, William Carlos Williams, there are "no ideas but in things."

Things can connect us with the universe. The food we eat everyday grows out of the earth with the necessary help of the sun which also provides us heat and light.

Things can reflect the beauty of God. That is why it is important to be surrounded by as much beauty as possible—house plants, the look of wood, a violin concerto by Brahms, a photograph by Thomas Eakins, etc. For Walt Whitman, "each precise object or condition or combination or process exhibits a beauty." Speaking of a bluebell, the English poet-priest, Gerard Manley Hopkins wrote, "I know the beauty of the Lord by it." Annie Dillard, in *Pilgrim at Tinker Creek* (New York: Bantam, 1974), saw the common things around her with such precision and clarity that the whole world became an epiphany or manifestation of God.

Things can take us outside of ourselves. This is an important need of all of us, particularly in these times of much introspection, psychologizing, and self-analysis. When we realize the beauty and magnificence of something, we feel small and not so stuck in our usual perceptions. Watching a sunrise or sunset or walking in a city park or a woods can be a transforming and healing experience.

It is not surprising that St. John Chrysostom (b. 347-d. 407) said in a sermon to parents on the right way to bring up a child, "Show him the sky, the sun, the flowers of the earth, meadows, and fair books. Let these give pleasure to his eyes. . . ." The first thing that many spiritual directors suggest to those who ask their help in prayer is that they try to look closely at and listen to concrete things outside of themselves.

Twentieth century philosopher, Martin Heidegger claims that people today have lost contact with real things. Reflecting Heidegger on this point, Arne Naess, a Norwegian interpreter of his, writes: "The horrifying thing is not the latest doomsday weapon but the fact that nothing any-more is near to us, that things no longer appear for us, essentially, in their illuminating fullness."

The problem is that many people live in a world of abstractions, ideologies, expectations, and devoid of real things. They attribute little or no value to things in themselves (cars, clothes, houses, etc.), but only to what they get out of them (attention, praise, status, confidence, etc.). In other words, things are owned, not because of what they are, but because of what they confer on us. In "dangling conversations," many people give each other opinions and superficial sighs which Paul Simon says are "the borders of our lives." They do not give touches, eye-to-eye glances, and real feelings. Simon again, ". . . I only kiss your shadow, I cannot feel your hand." They "kill each other with abstractions" by stereotypes, expectations, sermons, and other "trips" which don't fit. They are not materialist enough because they don't really see and feel the material things around them.

Another manifestation of the problem is that instead of possessing things, sometimes things possess us. Our houses and apartments are cluttered with things that we do not use or appreciate. Our shopping centers are filled with people who are buying things not because they need them but because they are feeling sorry for themselves or because they are bored. For many people, the things they possess constitute themselves and their identity. For such a person: I am equals what I have. The late Erich Fromm calls this a manifestation of "the having mode of existence." More simple living with less things around us will mean a greater presence to the things that remain.

Heidegger wrote, "For the way to what is near is always the longest and thus the hardest for us humans."

One way to counter the problem of living in a world of abstractions and being possessed by possessions is to make prolonged acts of communion with concrete things around you: a tree, a painting, a pebble. Look closely at it. Be present to it. Get "into it" and outside of yourself.

The principle that a person must "find God in all things" is central not only to the theology of St. Ignatius but also to the experience of anyone who finds God in everyday life.

Par Lagerkvist wrote, "One for whom a pebble has value must be surrounded by treasures wherever he goes."

Jesus said, "Look at the birds in the sky. . . . Think of the flowers growing in the fields . . ." (Matthew 6:26).

Questions for Reflection

1. What things in your daily life do you value most?

2. To what degree are you able to be present to things?

3. How developed is your sense of perception? How well and deeply are you able to see things?

4. To what extent are you influenced by expectations, abstractions, distractions, and preconceived experiences?

5. Do you ever experience "communication" between yourself and material things?

6. When was the last time that you remember a thing taking you outside of yourself?

7. Reflect on a recent experience of a prolonged act of communion with some concrete thing around you.

Bibliography

Buber, Martin, *Hasidism and Modern Man* (New York: Harper & Row, 1966), $2.50 paperback.
This is a book of Hasidic spirituality. The 1st and 2nd sections consist of a thematic and autobiographical interpretation of Hasidism; the 3rd, written in 1908, considers the themes of ecstasy, service, intention, and humility in the life of the Hasidim; the 4th, written in 1948, consists of six sections, each in the form of a commentary on an Hasidic tale; the 5th is a commentary on quotations from the Baal-Shem, the founder of Hasidism; the 6th is an essay on the relation of religion and ethics. "Hasidism, as Buber portrays it, is a mysticism which hallows community and every day life . . ."

Cardenal, Ernesto, *To Live Is To Love* (Garden City: Doubleday, 1974), $1.45 paperback.
This book is a series of reflections on the interior life. The author, who wrote "All things speak to us of God, because all things sigh for God . . ." tries to open the reader's eyes to the reality that all beings love one another by their very co-existence. A main theme: through the stuff of life God's continuing presence in and with all creation is made clear. "God surrounds us everywhere with beauty and poetry, placing within our reach through the media of our eyes and of all our bodily senses the visible beauty which He has created and which is a shining mirror of His Invisible Beauty."

Capon, Robert Farrar, *An Offering of Uncles* (New York: Sheed and Ward, 1967), $3.95 hardback. Out of print.
Subtitled "The Priesthood of Adam & the Shape of the World," this work tries "to refresh the sense of the priesthood of Adam, to lift up once more the idea of man as the priest of creation, as the offerer, the interceder, the seizer of its shape and the agent of its history." The book consists

39

of essays on the themes of place, time, history, mystery, material things, the body, and family, among others. This work reflects Capon's conviction that the human person was meant "not simply to be the lover of beauty, but the lover of being, just because it is."

Teilhard de Chardin, *Hymn of the Universe* (New York: Harper & Row, 1969), $3.50 paperback.

This book consists of four sections in the form of prose poems under the headings of: Mass Over the World, Christ in the World of Matter, The Spiritual Power of Matter, and Thoughts. The scientist-priest author conveys both his reverence for the material world and his constant awareness of God's presence felt throughout the created world. The author prays, "I thank you, my God, for having in a thousand different ways led my eyes to discover the immense simplicity of things."

5   *Making a Day*

If your daily life seems poor, do not blame it; blame
yourself, tell yourself that you are not poet enough to
call forth its riches.*

It is within the power of each person to make a day.

Usually people see a day as a "given," something over
which they have little or no control, a chronological mea-
surement of time. A day just happens to people who see it
this way.

When a person lets a day happen to her, she is domi-
nated by time in a chronological sense: clock-time, a system
of measuring duration. When a person makes her own day,
she sees time in a biblical sense, as *kairos,* a period of, almost a call to, feeling possibilities and making decisions.
Something important is going on.

Whether a day just happens to us or whether we make
it is our choice. We are cause, not effect.

Henry David Thoreau learned this when he went to
Walden Pond. "I went to the woods because I wished to
live deliberately . . . and not, when I came to die, discover
that I had not lived." Living deliberately is making a day.

*These words were written in the first years of this century by the German
poet, Rainer Maria Rilke, in a book of ten letters which he wrote to a young
friend, *Letters to a Young Poet* (New York: W. W. Norton & Company, 1954),
p. 19.

Thoreau called affecting the quality of a day "the highest of arts." He wrote, "It is something to be able to paint a particular picture, or to carve a statue . . . but it is far more glorious to carve and paint the very atmosphere and medium through which we look . . . which morally we can do."

The character Uncle Murray, in Herb Gardner's play, *A Thousand Clowns*, tells his nephew, "You got to know what day it is. . . . You have to own your days and name them, each one of them, or else the years go right by and none of them belongs to you." Owning and naming your days is the same thing as making them.

The greatest Jewish philosopher and theologian of the 20th century, Martin Buber, claimed that reality is new everyday and that every morning it asks anew to be shaped by our hands. The more complex our society and lives are, the more need there is to make our days. Artists are people who give shape to the chaos of the material with which they are working. We are all artists in the power we have to make our days.

Making a day means, more than anything else, taking responsibility for the right components being part of it. Though it sounds corny, it is similar to baking a cake: the quality of the cake depends on the right ingredients being in it. The quality of a day depends on the right ingredients. This calls for planning, prioritizing components, blending parts together sometimes, and disciplining oneself to see that this all happens. This is not as difficult as it sounds. There's a lot to be said for healthy patterns and habits in our daily rituals. They can facilitate the process considerably while saving us both time and energy.

What are the right components of a good day?

They will vary somewhat from person to person. They will vary in terms of the particular responsibilities in each person's life. This writer tries to make every day in his life contain the following ingredients:

1. *Work.* Samuel Johnson was probably right when he

said that a man must find happiness in his work or he won't find it at all. How does this apply, though, to the many people in our society today who don't seem to be finding happiness in their work? There is a great need in this country for work to be done well: among others, clerks who know what they are selling, people in gas stations who know something about cars, teachers who can make learning exciting to students because it is exciting to themselves, and priests who can listen to people and be a part of their lives to a degree that they can give good homilies. Some people give work an exaggerated place by not being able to stop working (men are particularly prone to being workaholics) or talking shop, by attributing almost religious qualities to work, or by not developing the ability to play.

2. *Play.* The book of Ecclesiasticus says, "When it is time to leave, tarry not; be off for home! There take your ease, and there enjoy doing as you wish . . ." (32:11–12). God calls us to play as to work. Play is an art that many adults lost when they left childhood. Aristotle saw virtue in play and praised the *eutrapelos,* the persons who were able to turn deeds or words into relaxation. Down deep some people are suspicious of play, pleasure, and sensuality. They feel a little bit guilty when they are having a good time. Others don't know how to have a good time in a social situation. Going to a party, for them, is more like work than play. We adults need to find again and nourish the child within us. We need to learn how to play again. This ability is not unrelated to the spiritual life and to celebrating good liturgies.

3. *Togetherness and aloneness.* These ingredients are not the opposites that they might appear to be on first sight. They come together and feed each other. To be with others in satisfying ways a person must be alone at times; to be alone peacefully a person must be enriched by being with others. Still, the greater need today is for people to be alone more often and more peacefully. Rabbi Moshe Leib

43

wrote, "A human being who has not a single hour for his own everyday is no human being." The philosopher Alfred North Whitehead wrote that religion is what a person does with his or her aloneness.

4. *Physical exercise.* Our bodies are more than containers of our souls. We are our bodies. Fortunate the person for whom physical exercise through work or chores is a regular part of his or her daily life. Otherwise, specific time—five to ten minutes, at a minimum—should be given each day to exercise. It tones the body, raises consciousness, gives energy, and is a kind of therapy. A person does not need to embark upon a time-consuming exercise program and buy expensive equipment to accomplish this.

Taking a vigorous half-hour walk each day is excellent exercise and much more. A simple walk assists the digestion of food, helps to control weight, provides an effective outlet for nervous tension, and stimulates the imagination. Some brisk walking every day actually lowers blood pressure and pulse rate and sustains the heart muscle in healthy tone. Hal Borland writes, "All walking is discovery. On foot we take the time to see things whole." Learning to walk again, something many Americans need to do, means realizing and overcoming our addiction-dependency on cars. The physical exercise of walking is not limited just to the physical realm: it has much to do with both our psychological and spiritual lives. An ordinary walk can have a lot to do with making a good day.

5. *Prayer.* The next chapter will deal exclusively with this ingredient.

6. *Contact with the natural world.* Nature possesses healing powers when we truly experience it. Buckminster Fuller writes that we need to find out what nature is doing so that we can be in harmony with it. Nature takes us outside of ourselves, provides us with the food of symbolic consciousness, and restores us. Some Old Testament psalmists were inspired to praise God through their contact with

the natural world. Visiting nearby city parks, camping out, backpacking hikes, observing and taking care of house plants, and being present to the magical moments of dawn and dusk are some common ways of making contact with the natural world that can be integrated easily into an ordinary day.

7. *Silence.* We live in such a noisy culture. The noise of cars, constructions, and media seems to be almost everywhere. We need silence to get our inner messages, to be reflective, and to give value to our talking. French philosopher Gabriel Marcel wrote that it is in silence that we should seek the native soil in which faith can grow. European essayist Max Picard, in his neglected little classic, *The World of Silence* (Chicago: Regnery, 1961) wrote, "Real speech is in fact nothing but the resonance of silence" and "There is more silence than language in love."

There is something religious about the act of putting together a day with all the right ingredients. Such a well-made day, in itself, is a prayer and helps the one who does it to live in the presence of God.

Morning usually has everything to do with the rest of the day. The person who makes his or her own days usually appreciates morning in a special way. This person knows that the quality of a morning depends on the rest and sleep of the night before. For many, morning is the time when silence and aloneness are most available to them. It might well be the only time that they are.

The famous Dutch catechism for adults, *A New Catechism* (New York: Herder & Herder, 1967), states that early morning is a privileged time for prayer. "Many of us would be happier if we got up half an hour earlier and went more quietly about everything each day. The morning hours are golden. And prayer is part of this gold."

Morning brings a new day, one that can be made differently from the day before. That description of morning says a lot about both God and us.

45

Questions for Reflection

1. What is your common experience of daily life?

2. Do you feel that it is within your power to make your days?

3. How often do you let days just happen to you?

4. What are the right components that would be part of an ideal day for you?

5. What is your relationship to work and to play?

6. How much and what kind of physical exercise do you get each day or each week?

7. What are the ordinary ways that you make contact with the world of nature?

Bibliography

Durckheim, Karlfried, *Daily Life As Spiritual Exercise* (New York: Harper & Row, 1971), $1.45 paperback. *This book aims to show that daily life, especially its routine, can be used as a perpetual opportunity to practice the "Way" and can itself be lived as a spiritual exercise. The author emphasizes the possibilities of posture, tension, breathing, and gesture and suggests five steps in the process of transformation: critical awareness, letting go, union, new-becoming, and testing the new form in daily life. "No matter what we are doing—walking, standing or sitting, writing, speaking or being silent, attacking something or defending ourselves, helping or serving others—whatever the task, it is possible to carry it out with a posture and an at-*

titude that will more and more establish the contact with being.''

Edwards, Tilden, *Living Simply Through the Day* (New York: Paulist Press, 1977) $5.95 paperback.
The premise of this book by an Episcopal priest is that attentive living is our spirituality. After autobiographical reflections, the author develops the theme of simple presence throughout the day by reflecting on waking, praying, relating, serving, eating, playing, aching, and sleeping. Throughout he suggests practical processes for cultivating attentiveness in each daily activity.

Rahner, Karl, *"Everyday Things"* in *Belief Today* (New York: Sheed and Ward, 1967), $3.50 hardback.
The premise of this 43-page section of the book is that "the very commonness of everyday things harbors the eternal marvel and silent mystery of God and his grace and retains them only so long as it retains it commonness." Because little things have unutterable depths, the author reflects on work, getting about, sitting down, seeing, laughter, eating, sleep, and grace in everyday life.

Scott-Moncrieff, George, *This Day* (London: Hollis & Carter, 1959).
The author presents parts of the day as metaphors for different stages in the spiritual life: sons of the morning, the noonday devil, the long afternoon, and the cool of evening. Richard of St. Victor spoke of the transformation of the Christian into Christ as a progress from dawn to full day. Emphasis is given to living in the present. "Yet in the light of God's will nothing is humdrum, for the present moment holds the sacramental significance of the divine presence." It would be unfortunate if this fine little book passes out of print while it is largely unknown in the United States.

6 *Paying Attention to Everyday Life*

In prayer we discover what we already have. You start
where you are and you deepen what you already have.
And you realize that you are already there. We already
have everything, but we don't know it and we don't
experience it. Everything has been given to us in
Christ. All we need is to experience what we already
possess. The trouble is we aren't taking time to do so.*

Prayer is more listening than speaking. And listening
in almost any situation is a hard thing for most of us to do.

God speaks to us, the most important dimension of
prayer, through each other, the newspaper, joys, problems,
the Church, our own reflecting, the Bible, nothingness, the
sacraments, our bodies, and the natural/social world. All
that we need to do is to pay attention and listen.

This is hard to do because most people are very often
in the action mode of living: acting on the world and doing
things to objects to bring about possession and relief from
pain. There is nothing wrong with this mode and, much of
the time, it is appropriate. Still, it is not the only way of liv-

*These words were spoken by Thomas Merton to Cistercian nuns at Red-
woods Abbey in northern California on the eve of his historic flight to the Orient,
the journey on which he died. Quoted by M. Basil Pennington, O.C.S.O. in *Centering Prayer,* they are some of the last words of this great spiritual teacher.

ing. In the receptive mode, which is another way, people take in, receive, and unify. Letting things and people be or allowing them to be is the essence of the receptive mode. Praying is in greater harmony with the receptive mode than the action mode. The main reason that prayer is difficult for some people is that the action mode has become their norm, their way of life.

To pray is to listen. Listen? Listen. Listen. Be there. Be here and now. Pay attention. Observe well. Reflect. Mull over. Discuss. Fret. See deeply. Connect. Listen. Revise. Praise. Give thanks. Then keep listening.

The position of limiting God's word to the church, the Pope, priests, the seven sacraments, and formal prayer (the temptation for Roman Catholics) and to the Bible (the temptation for Protestants) is an effective way to partially silence God. He—though God is beyond our categories of "he" and "she"—speaks to us also in our everyday lives.

Prayer is paying attention to our everyday lives. Our speaking to God is the smaller part of praying. God speaking to us is the greater part.

Roman Catholics, for the most part, are used to certain specific forms of prayer: the Mass, the Hail Mary, the Our Father, the Rosary, the Act of Contrition, etc. When these classic ways of talking to God are connected with our real lives, they are powerful indeed.

Still, there are many other ways to pray. Each person needs to discover and "sink into" the forms of prayer that are the most natural expression for her. Dom Chapman wrote, "Pray as you can, don't pray as you can't." Each person needs to find ways to pray which fit with his or her temperament, personality, schedule, and other responsibilities. Prayer is not so complex or difficult that all forms of it will conflict with the practical reality of people and their lives. The person who thinks this has a narrow understanding of prayer and has yet to find the forms that can be in an easy, natural harmony with her.

49

Here are four ways of praying to consider:

1. *Prayer as a qualitative response to life.* The quality with which we do whatever it is that we are doing (being parents, going to classes, spending time with a friend, working in a factory or office, preparing and eating a meal, etc.), is a form of prayer. This approach grounds prayer in our real lives.

Jewish prayer is centered around life. Jesus was a Jew so his emphasis on the connection between prayer and life is not surprising. Jesus found many different ways to listen to his Father: going off by himself for prayer in the stillness and quiet of the night, watching attentively shepherds caring for their sheep, the flowing quality of the Jordan River, the faces of people who gathered around him, studying his Hebrew Scriptures, and talking with his friends and followers. Theologian Robert Funk writes, "Jesus without saying so, by his very way of presenting man, shows that for him man's destiny is at stake in his ordinary creaturely existence, domestic, economic, and social."

In what is probably the best recent book on adult prayer, *On Becoming a Musical Mystical Bear* (New York: Paulist Press, 1976), Dominican theologian, Matthew Fox writes, "To enjoy life is to say Thank You for it." Perhaps some people should try to get "unstuck" from attitudes and patterns which get in the way of their enjoyment of life. Fox also stresses that social action or working to improve the world is a form of prayer. Responding to life—by enjoying it and by shaping it—is responding to the Creator of life. We pray when we experience our life as a gift. This form of prayer is related to the theology behind the Morning Offering.

Praying as a qualitative response to life is common among people who do not look upon it as prayer and criticize themselves for not praying more often.

2. *Praying as reading the Bible.* One of the really exciting things happening these days in Catholic lives is a new

appreciation of the Bible. Many Catholics are coming to know the Bible as prayer, something that many Protestants have known for a long time. The Bible becomes a prayer when the person reading it discovers or makes a connection between the passage being read and his life.

Spiritual writer Louis Evely looks upon Scripture as a revelation of what is happening in our lives. Evely finds the Gospel to be "passionately interesting" because he experiences it as talking about himself. He writes, "I see my life in the light of the Gospel, but I also read the Gospel in the light of my life. . . . What they (the evangelists) tell me helps me to understand my own experiences more clearly, and my own experience helps me to understand their message . . . Try taking this as a guiding rule for interpreting the Scriptures: everything they tell happens in your life, everything that happens in your life is prophesied, lived in the Scriptures."

The Liturgy of the Word at Mass can become significantly more meaningful if a person (or couple or family) would look over and discuss the three biblical readings during the week before Sunday. During this reflection and discussion throughout the week, connections can be made between the readings and daily life. If this is done, the impact of the readings will not depend so much on the quality of the homily, an aspect of the liturgy about which there seems to be widespread dissatisfaction. When the Liturgy of the Word is experienced as full of meaning, then the whole Mass will become a more real and satisfying celebration.

3. *Praying as meditation.* Most of our minds, most of the time, are filled with clutter of various sorts: psychological games, expectations, worries, regrets, defenses, anxiety, etc. This clutter frequently prevents us from really being where we are. T. S. Eliot wrote that people in modern times are "distracted from distractions by distractions."

Meditation is a way out of mental clutter and distractions. It is a way of emptying or clearing the mind of all the

51

busyness usually going on there and simply being present. This is objectless meditation and it is quite similar to Transcendental meditation (TM) and Zen meditation *(zazen)*. When fundamentalists look on this type of meditation as unchristian, they reveal their ignorance of its longtime presence in the Christian tradition which also has emphasized discursive meditation, the mind using concepts and images to reflect on the mysteries of Christ. In *Centering Prayer: Renewing an Ancient Christian Prayer Form* (Garden City: Doubleday, 1980), Trappist monk M. Basil Pennington documents the constant presence of objectless meditation in the Christian tradition and describes some other forms of it: the *Cloud of the Unknowing* prayer, the way of inner silence, the practice of loving attentiveness, prayer of the heart, prayer of quiet, and centering prayer.

What is necessary to meditate in this manner? A situation in which you will not be disturbed. A relaxed posture which usually means that the back is in an upright position. A mind which lets go, empties itself of clutter, and watches itself slow down. Eyes that really see (though it is also possible to meditate with eyes closed), ears that really hear, and a touch that registers every vibration.

One should not try too hard to empty the mind or fight the thoughts that will come up inevitably. If you resist them, they will persist. Anything that comes to mind should simply be let in and out with no effort to get rid of it. This meditation should be done on an empty stomach (so your body can assist the process and not be busy digesting food at the time) for twenty minutes before breakfast and/or bedtime.

This formal period of meditation can influence the rest of the day by helping the one doing it to realize her degree of presence in any situation and the flowing quality of any experience. Letting go, another way to describe meditation, helps the meditator to let things and other people be. A Zen poem sums it up: Sitting quietly, doing nothing, spring comes, and the grass grows by itself.

Some people, almost always those who have not experienced it, ask why this form of meditation is considered a prayer. It is prayer because God is revealed in the letting be of being. A person doesn't have to take expensive courses or college classes to learn to meditate. Disciplining himself by practicing it regularly is all that is necessary. In the beginning it won't be easy because the posture might be painful and the twenty minutes might seem endless. Before too long, though, the person practicing it regularly will realize that he taught himself to meditate just by doing it.

4. *Praying as listening to yourself.* Prayer usually is seen as reaching out, turning away from oneself and daily life, and stretching toward God. The theology implicit in this form of prayer usually locates God "out there" in the heavens, related in an external way to human history and the community of humankind.

Theologian Gregory Baum describes another model of prayer which has a different inner structure. "Instead of reaching out beyond himself, the Christian in his inner concentration remains close to the ordinary things of life, tries to be in touch with himself, with all of himself . . . to open himself to the deepest dimension of his being. To pray to God means to remain where we are, to lay hold of what is there, to pass through the superficial layers to the profound meaning. To pray is to be in touch with oneself in a new way: to listen to the melody, not made by ourselves, that sounds at the core of our being."

This form of prayer does not remove us from everyday life but drives us more deeply into it. God is not in the heavens but in the depths of our persons, our lives, and our world.

My former, wonderful spiritual director, Msgr. C. F. Griffith, to whom this book is dedicated, used to tell the seminarians at St. Ambrose College in a way that was hard to forget, "If you are too busy to pray, you are too busy." Every day should include some sort of prayer. When a person recognizes the wide variety of prayer forms available, any excuse for not praying regularly becomes invalid.

Our culture is noisy, full of various messages and voices shouting at us most of the time. God usually doesn't shout. Just the opposite. His voice and style are more like a gentle spring breeze.

Notice. Pay attention. Listen.

Questions for Reflection

1. On a scale of one to ten, how do you rate your ability to listen to yourself? to others?

2. When do you experience being in the receptive mode of living?

3. Do you discover the Word of God not only in the Bible but in other places also? What other places for you?

4. What forms of prayer are the most natural expressions for you?

5. How often do you experience your mind emptied or cleared of the clutter that is there most of the time? When?

6. What excuses do you give to yourself for not praying more often? Reflect on them and evaluate them.

7. What are the factors that get in the way of your experiencing what you already possess?

Bibliography

Abhishiktananda (Henri Le Saux, O.S.B.) *Prayer* (Philadelphia: Westminster Press, 1972), $1.95 paperback.
A priest of the Benedictine Order, the author has completely identified himself with the people of India and lives as one of their holy men. The basic premise is that to live in the presence of God should be as natural for a Christian as to breathe the air which surrounds him. This book describes several different forms of prayer. "To look with eyes enlightened by faith at trees and plants, at fruits and flowers, at birds and animals—all of them created by the Father to help and serve ̄us and to be used by us in our ascent towards him—is also nothing less than prayer and contemplation."

Lassalle, H. M. Enomiya, *Zen Meditation for Christians* (LaSalle: Open Court, 1974), $9.95 hardback.
This book describes Zen meditation, the classical Oriental art of going beyond conscious thought, and draws remarkable parallels to Christian mysticism. A Jesuit priest, the author believes that the way of Zen does not conflict theologically with Christian belief and shows how Zen meditation can be used by Christians to heighten their understanding of God. The book describes ways to empty the mind, slow the stream of consciousness until it ceases altogether, focus the body in the lotus position, and then await enlightenment through the paradox of nothingness.

Nhat, Hanh Thich, *The Miracle of Mindfulness* (Boston: Beacon Press, 1976) $3.95 paperback.
Subtitled "A Manual on Meditation," this book describes mindfulness as keeping one's consciousness alive to the present reality and presents many practical exercises to help integrate mindfulness with daily life. Meditation is to be

practiced constantly as an integral part of our involvement in all ordinary tasks. Mindfulness is the life of awareness and means the presence of life. "Every day we are engaged in a miracle which we don't even recognize: a blue sky, white clouds, green leaves, the black, curious eyes of a child—our own two eyes. All is a miracle."

Schmidt, Joseph F., *Praying Our Experiences* (Winona: St. Mary's College Press, 1980), $1.95 paperback.

"Praying our experiences" is the practice of reflecting on and entering honestly into the day-to-day events of our lives to become aware of God's Word in them. The book describes sincere reflection on our experience as a way of prayer and then applies this approach to self-knowledge, introspection, healing the past, writing, scripture, ministry, and faith. "We pray our experiences when we use the content of our lived existence as the content of our prayer."

7 *Transforming Everyday Life*

Then I heard a loud voice call from the throne, 'you see this city? Here God lives among men. He will make his home among them; they shall be his people, and he will be their God; his name is God-with-them. He will wipe away all tears from their eyes; there will be no more death, and no more mourning or sadness. The world of the past has gone.*

Then the One sitting on the throne spoke: 'Now I am making the whole of creation new!'*

It is not hyperbole—exaggeration for effect—to say that we are all artists and poets. Even the most unimaginative and uncreative person among us makes his or her own world.

Each person makes herself to be the person that she is. This is the most profound artistic activity possible. Each person struggles to find the precise words which accurately describe what he sees and feels. This is basically the poet's work.

Because of the risen Christ, each of us has the power to transform our everyday lives: to find the extraordinary in

---

*These words are from the book of Revelation, Chapter 21:3–5.

the ordinary or to make transparent what is opaque. When something is experienced as opaque, we see it, use it, and then see what William Blake called this "single vision." When something is experienced as transparent, we see it and then we see through it to deeper meanings.

A story and some concrete examples might help to make clear what is meant by the transformation of everyday life. In 1915 the Anglican authority on mysticism, Evelyn Underhill wrote the following story about two people named Eyes and No-Eyes in her book, *Practical Mysticism* (New York: Dutton, 1943):

No-Eyes has fixed his attention on the fact that he is obliged to take a walk. For him the chief factor of existence is his own movement along the road; a movement which he intends to accomplish as efficiently and comfortably as he can. He asks not to know what may be on either side of the hedges. He ignores the caress of the wind until it threatens to remove his hat. He trudges along, steadily, diligently; avoiding the muddy pools, but oblivious of the light which they reflect.

Eyes takes the walk too: and for him it is a perpetual revelation of beauty and wonder. The sunlight inebriates him, the winds delight him, the very effort of the journey is a joy. Magic presences throng the roadside, or cry salutations to him from the hidden fields. The rich world through which he moves lies in the foreground of his consciousness; and it gives up new secrets to him at every step.

No-Eyes, when told of Eyes' adventures, usually refuses to believe that both have gone by the same road. He fancies that his companion has been floating about in the air, or beset by agreeable hallucinations. We shall never persuade him to the contrary unless we persuade him to look for himself.

This story describes how Eyes experiences life as transparent and No-Eyes experiences life as opaque.

Some other examples. Take our bodies. Our bodies can be just there, carriers of our souls, considered unimportant, not taken care of, and hardly even noticed. Or they can be experienced as who we are, as overwhelmingly beautiful, even miraculous in their working, something to be taken care of, a connection to the ground and the universe, a marvelous gift from God. (The psalmist prayed, "I give you thanks that I am . . . wonderfully made": Psalm 139.)

Take food. It can be just something to keep us going, a hassle to buy and prepare, processed and filled with chemicals, preservatives, and dyes, and taken for granted. Or it can be a reminder of our connection to the earth, the source of constant pleasure, constituent of who we are (it is true that, to some extent, we are what we eat), an expression of love and friendship, and a reason to give thanks to God.

Take meeting another person. It can be routine, a superficial experience, a chance for ego gratification, an exercise in manipulation, and a "downer." Or it can be filled with possibilities, a way to get outside of ourselves, a chance to learn and see beauty (for nothing, not even the world of nature, is as beautiful as the human person), and the context for experiencing the presence of God.

Of course, everything cannot be transparent all the time and some things are quite appropriately opaque. Still, if our lives are to be richer, more satisfying, and full of meaning—in short, more religious—then we need to bring more transparence to them.

Teilhard de Chardin wrote, "He Who Is dwells everywhere. It is only a matter of learning to look into the profound sphere of things, *of everything.* The secret of the world lies wherever we can discern the transparency of the universe. We could say in fact that the great mystery of

Christianity lies not in the appearance of God in the universe but in his transparence in it."

The risen Christ, whom we celebrate in a focused way on Easter and on every Sunday, is both the supreme model and the powerful source of transformation.

The Resurrection means the transformation of the Jesus of history into the Christ of faith. Christ lives now in a new sort of way. Many people are surprised to hear that Christ today is still a man and that his new life is a human life. He is still humanly conscious with his consciousness being a continuation of the one he had before his death. He still possesses human affectivity which continues the human affection he had before his death.

Christ's new risen life, glorifying the Father and interceding for us, is a transformation of his old life. The Resurrection and Ascension are about transformation and not geographical distance (from here to there).

Nothing is exactly the same since the Resurrection. Today Christ continues to transform all reality and we who follow Christ are called to be intimately involved in that process. In short, we are called to "make the whole of creation new." That is why we need to know the risen Christ (not just the historical Jesus) and realize that his continuing humanity is the basis of his profound identification with us.

Theologian Gerald O'Collins, S.J., writes, "The Resurrection is seen as nothing less than the great artist discovering and disengaging our hidden body of glory." To discover and disengage our hidden body of glory in the world is to transform everyday life: what is extraordinary is seen and experienced in the ordinary. The Resurrection and the Ascension are not Christ's departure from his disciples but his lasting presence to them—and to us.

Suspect and neglected though it is, the imagination is the main faculty by which we make our lives transparent and transform our everyday world. This is why William

Blake considered it to be a religious power. Theologians today are starting again to take the imagination seriously. Gregory Baum defines faith as that which happens when Jesus rules the imagination. He writes, "Jesus then is *that through which* we experience ourselves and other people." The life of a believer is transparent and transformed.

The state of the imagination of individuals and communities is a key religious issue. Individuals need imagination to discover connections between the risen Christ and our world today. Communities need imagination to perceive real human needs, decide upon priorities, and then effectively respond to the needs. When parents read fairy tales and similar literature to children, they are assisting significantly in the development of their imaginations. This is probably a more fundamental and lasting religious education for their children than dozens of religion classes and liturgies.

The emphasis in this book has been on finding God in everyday life. What Johannes Tauler, a mystic in the 15th century, said is true, "Who does not seek and find and receive God at home, or in the street, will never receive him rightly in church, that is certain."

Still, this emphasis does not make Sunday, sacraments, and formal prayer any less important. It is ironic and true that, with this emphasis, they are all the more important.

The focused moments of sacramental celebration, the Bible, and formal prayer clarify and intensify for us what is going on all the time in our everyday lives. God is feeding us constantly with the "bread" of daily life—the "bread" which is our families and friends, our work and our world. We eat the bread of the Eucharistic celebration to remind us of the feeding which is going on all the time. Being forgetful, distracted, and ungrateful much of the time, all manifestations of our sinfulness, we need this focus and clarification.

The ideal toward which we should strive is an experience of interplay between our everyday lives and the focused moments. They should both influence each other. Our daily lives should draw us to and give meaning to the focused moments which, in turn, should clarify and deepen our understanding and appreciation of what is going on all the time. The classics scholar, Norman O. Brown writes, "All meaning is in the interplay."

The risen Christ means that we can be new people, with new mornings, who go about making a new world. Of course, we are the same people, it's just another morning, and it's the same old world. Only now, with Christ saving us from "single vision," it is all transformed.

Questions for Reflection

1. In what ways do you make your own world and in what ways do you make yourself to be the person you are?

2. List and reflect on three different experiences in which you discovered the extraordinary in the ordinary.

3. When have you experienced your life as transparent?

4. Did you identify more with Eyes or No-Eyes?

5. Do you believe that Jesus Christ is still a man today with human consciousness and human affectivity?

6. How do you rate the state of your imagination?

7. Describe the interplay which happens or which you would like to make happen between your daily life and the Sunday Masses you celebrate.

Bibliography

Brown, Norman O., *Love's Body* (New York: Vintage, 1968), $1.95 paperback.
Brown's main concern is that we are too literal minded because we tend to understand things in only one way. Brown describes symbolic consciousness by a rich and diverse variety of aphoristic quotations on the themes of liberty, nature, trinity, unity, person, representative, head, boundary, food, fire, fraction, resurrection, fulfillment, judgment, freedom, and nothing. "To make in ourselves a new consciousness, an erotic sense of reality, is to become conscious of symbolism. Symbolism is mind making connections (correspondences) rather than distinctions (separations). Symbolism makes conscious interconnections and unions that were unconscious and repressed."

Howard, Thomas, *An Antique Drum* (Philadelphia: J. B. Lippincott: 1969), $2.95 paperback.
Subtitled "The World As Image," this book consists of fine reflections on myth and meaning, imagination, ritual, painting, moral life, sex, and transforming daily life. Imagination is described as the faculty by which we organize the content of our experience into some form and thus apprehend it as significant. ". . . the commonplaces of life, the given rhythms of experience in which every human being is involved are themselves the occasions in which we may enact what is real, what lies at the root of things. All this commonplace stuff is what life is really about . . . the failure to seize these humdrum commonplaces as vitally significant, or the effort to fly from them and seek fulfillment in various forms of substitution or diversion, represents a misapprehension of what it means to be authentically human."

Powers, Joseph, *Spirit and Sacrament* (New York: Seabury, 1973), $6.95 hardback.

This neglected work is an attempt at discovering what human experience the symbols of God, Spirit, the Christ, the Church of the Christ, the New Creation, the Body of the Lord should contain and produce. Its premise is that it is through the Spirit that the meaning of God and Jesus find their resonance within human experience. "What holiness does is not to deliver us from the ordinary facts of human existence, but to transform our very ordinary existence from within that ordinary existence."

Williams, H. A., *True Resurrection* (New York: Harper & Row, 1974), $2.45 paperback.

The Episcopal priest author views resurrection as the passage from death to life which we are able to experience in daily life. He describes it in relation to the body, mind, goodness, suffering, and death. "The miracle is to be found precisely within the ordinary round. . . . Resurrection occurs to us as we are, and its coming is generally quiet and unobtrusive and we may hardly be aware of its creative power."